This book belongs to

Hi, I'm Lucky.

People call me Lucky the Farting Leprechaun. Some people say I'm lucky because I escaped from a leprechaun trap not once, but twice!

How, you ask?

Well, let's just say farting is my magical superpower. And this specific superpower takes on many forms:

Knockout Key

When you've fallen for a trap and can't get out, a **knockout key** delivers the secret punch you need to get out of a pinch!

Rainbow Rocket

If you just escaped from your leprechaun trap, you've got to run! And a **rainbow rocket** is a perfect vehicle for the escape! This fart will take you to the moon and back. I just hop on and off I go!

Green Giant

A **green giant** happens when you let one out, but it's smell continues to grow stronger and stronger until it takes a hold of it's victims.

Potty Gold

When you have to go, you just have to go! These farts come at the best time - when you are all alone with just you and the **potty**.

Clever Four Leaf Clover

When I fart in a crowded room and no one knows it's me, it's called a **clever four leaf clover**. Since there are so many people, no one knows who did it which is pretty lucky!

Then, there are times when your tummy alerts you that something special is coming but then you find out it wasn't poop, it was just **fake gold**!

Leprechauns must exercise to stay fit. And one of our favorite exercises is the **Shamrock Salutation** with, of course, some gas to liven things up!

Bouncy Bagpipes

Have you ever been at a party and just let some farts out without a care in the world because the music is playing so loud? Those are called **bouncy bagpipes**!

Have you ever had this feeling? Your stomach starts to make rumbling sounds. Then you let one rip and it's the loudest thing you've ever heard. Then, you've done a **loud legend**!

Poot Pops

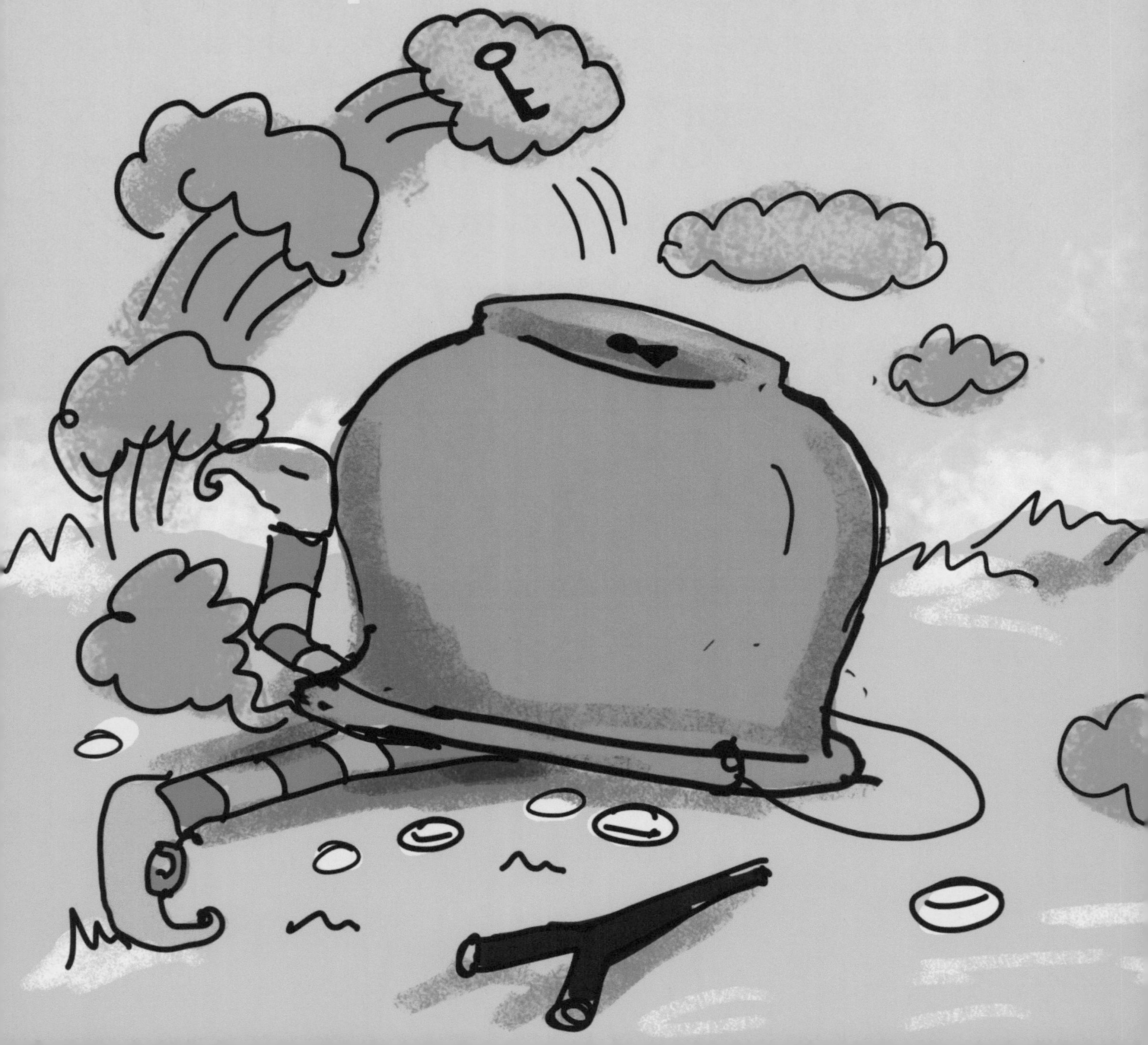

And last but not least, if you're trapped, just poot so you can pop yourself right out of the pot!

So if you ever get in a bind, just reach within!
We all have the **magic** within us!

If you don't believe me, just ask the Easter Bunny and refer to her Book of Bunny Farts.

To be continued....

Follow us on FB and IG @humorhealsus
To vote on new title names and freebies, visit
us at humorhealsus.com for more information.

@humorhealsus   @humorhealsus

CPSIA information can be obtained
at www.ICGtesting.com
Printed in the USA
BVHW021722230321
603277BV00010B/143